Flowers of Hope

Paula Ann Smith

WestBow Press books may be ordered through booksellers or by contacting:

WestBow Press
A Division of Thomas Nelson & Zondervan
1663 Liberty Drive
Bloomington, IN 47403
www.westbowpress.com
1 (866) 928-1240

ISBN: 978-1-4908-6382-5 (sc)
ISBN: 978-1-4908-6383-2 (e)

Library of Congress Control Number: 2014922328

Printed in the United States of America.

WestBow Press rev. date: 1/23/2015

WESTBOW
PRESS
A DIVISION OF THOMAS NELSON
& ZONDERVAN

To the sweetest man I ever knew; not only was he my friend, but he truly became my brother... Dick Laubach. To my sweet boys in Africa... it is because of you and your families that God and I have worked hand in hand to make it possible for others to receive blessing through the power of God, his great love and mercy. My prayer is that other hearts will be opened to the idea of sponsoring children like you through Compassion International or World Vision.

To Dirt Daubers for the beautiful garden at Mears and Main, it provided some sources for this book. As beautiful as it is from a car, it deserves a stop now and then for a personal stroll to see what new blossoms are blooming. Keep up the good work it is truly worth it. To my gal friends for the many ways you have backed me in this project. Through prayer and encouraging words and some hugs along the way, you have been my support system here on earth. To my family, you know who you are, thank you for the many ways we share life together. And, thank you God for putting us all together.

Ever wonder if God really exists? Just look to the flowers for answers. Do you see all the design that went into each and every one? That just didn't happen by some sheer coincidence. It happened by having a grand designer, a master creator. That's the handiwork of our Heavenly Father. You can see this handiwork in many things; animals, trees, the different landscapes all around the world. There really is some majestic scenery around the world! You can look at all these things and see that there is a grand designer.

There are more animals, more trees, more majestic landscapes, and yes, more flowers than any one person could see. Unless, of course, you study that field and travel the world. But, most of us will not have that option. And if that's not enough for you, look around every day of your life at all the different individual people you see. And remember there are thousands upon thousands more individual and unique people around the whole world.

This book just happens to be about some of the flowers in my small area of the world, where I live. As I grow older it's harder and harder to spend the hours in the garden that I use to do. There were times when I would go out at first light with a cup of coffee in hand, walk around the yard and plan out what I was doing that day. Then, just do garden work until late afternoon or early evening. Of course, those days are gone.

But my love of flowers and taking photos of them is not. If I had a camera in my hand before digital, I could blow through a roll of 36 exp. film in about 10-15 minutes. I can remember a day when I saw some cool bug on a leaf at the last garden from the house. Trust me my yard is not that big. I ran into the house to throw a new roll of film in the camera, just to get a photo of that bug on the leaf. When I went back outside, a flower in the closest garden caught my eye. So, I snapped photos as I worked my way out to the 2nd bed. To my delight the cool bug was still there on that leaf. But, to my dismay, I had no film left; when at last I made it to the cool bug. That's how fast I could burn through a roll of film. So you know how glad I am that we now have memory cards for our cameras. But, I still get the same feeling when it tells you the memory card is full. At least it takes so much longer now.

What I really want you to know is that there is a God. He not only created all these different and wonderful things in the world; He created us too. We don't have to go through life being in despair, being in grief, being in depression, being in financial strife, being at odds with your children, not understanding people at work. God is there for you always. You can commune with Him through prayer. And, if you're real quiet and you wait, you will get an answer. It could be a soft spoken word, it could come from someone being put in your path, it could be the look in a child's face. It could be the title of a book on a shelf, it could come from conversation with a friend or a message from a child, even if the child is all grown-up now.

Once a friend of mine called another friend and asked us to pray for her and her situation. When I ran out to my friend's car and got in, she told me about our friend's request for prayer. So we decided we would pray for her before we left my driveway. It was a gloomy day and I live in a neighborhood full of very tall trees. But as we prayed for our friend, a sunbeam broke through the clouds and shone through the front windshield and warmed our faces as we prayed. It brought tears to our eyes and we knew that prayer would be answered and our friend would be OK.

Those are the kinds of signs I am talking about. God shows us His presence every day; we just need to learn how to take the time to quiet ourselves and watch for them. They come in so many ways. If you cannot quiet yourself inside and are not really watching for things, those moments will pass you by and you will not ever realize it. There it was for you to see, but you may be too wrapped up in your own problems or issues that you just miss it. I know that I have done that very thing.

It could be the song of a bird or the way the wind blows leaves from the trees. One fall, my son had stopped over with his mulching lawnmower and mowed the yard, mulching up both grass and leaves. It was a beautiful fall day, but not long after he left the wind kicked up and the leaves began to fall. I went out the back door and looked up. Yes, you may have guessed it. I ran back in for my camera because it was raining leaves. I had never noticed the leaves coming down in just that special way. Be on the lookout for these special signs from God and you too will feel His presence.

I prayed at the altar, "God, what is it you wish for me to do for you? What is my path you have planned for me? Let me know Lord, I am ready to do your work." I prayed that prayer many times at the altar, but I was always eager to get back to my seat. My pastor tells us to wait at the altar. Don't be so anxious to leave after your prayer request. Quiet yourself and wait for God to answer.

One day I did just that, I waited at the altar. I fully put myself in that prayer and waited. I figured God would tell me something great that I could do to help my fellow man. Maybe I could be a guidance counselor; but no, I have no training for that. In fact, how could I help people when I was coming out of a 6 year depression after the death of my boyfriend? Who am I to help people? I was the one that had to be dragged out of my house to go shopping, dinner, and a movie with my friend. She invited me to go to a church her sister had asked her to go to. Ironically, it happened to be the same church that one of our bosses at work had invited us to go visit.

Once I attended that church, God began to work in me. I prayed for His help to get physically healthy. But God, in his all knowing wisdom, knew I needed the help with depression first. Every day step by step He brings me that much closer to being part of life again. I love the Lord, I know He is my Savior, my friend and my teacher. 'Through Him I can do All Things'

Well, to say the least, I was quite shocked at the altar. My word received from God wasn't to take some position at church and really work with people. You know we all do it, our minds work past God. We come up with our own ideas of what He's going to ask us to do. We don't wait we just rush on ahead in our anxiousness to do something good. We are smart enough to know all the answers and figure it out for ourselves. And, oh boy, do we figure it out for ourselves and sometimes we land ourselves in huge predicaments in our lives by thinking we have all the answers.

My word from God, my path I am supposed to follow, the thing he wants me to do for him, PHOTOGRAPHY. What?! That's my hobby, Lord, how is that going to help YOU? I am not a master photographer. I just take photos of what interests me. Flowers are probably my number one thing that I have taken photos of over all the years I've owned my own camera.

Yes, I must confess, it's OK, the Lord already knows. When I was a young child of 6 or 7 years old, living in Texas, before our family moved to Michigan, I stole one of those old fashioned cameras from a party at my grandmother's home. You know the ones that you flip the top up and look down into, I just had to have it! Well, I was promptly driven back to grandma's to confess my sin of what I had done. So, I guess I always had the passion for the camera from an early age. Another passion is flowers.

I began to wonder how to accomplish this path God gave me; it cannot be to take photos of people in church. One, my photos with my old camera of people weren't half bad for an amateur. But, with my digital, I am terrible at taking photos of people. I tried to take photos inside a church in Houston; of a play my uncle was in. To my dismay they were terrible and that was with my old camera.

But I started to think ahead of God again. Better sign up for a bunch of photography classes and get some real knowledge about it. But then my human mind slowed down and I realized God didn't ask me to do that. He just asked me to do photography, period, nothing more, nothing less.

He did put an idea in my head for a book of photography. That one is going to take me a little bit of time to put together. He's given me some ideas of it here and there. But the time is not right.

There has been this nagging feeling that things are taking too long for me to get busy and get started on His request. There's been no real direction except that I have felt as if there was something else I needed to do first. God, in his great wisdom, finds a way to put you on a path where He wants you to be. But back to the real reason of this book…

Our God is an almighty God, He is with us always! He's with us in the car, with us at home, with us at work, with us at school, with us in the store. He is with us everywhere we are. Not only is He with each of us where we are, He's also with everyone else around the world. He can be there for you just like He is here for me. All you have to do is seek Him, draw nearer to God and He will draw nearer to you.

He can be there to help you with whatever your problems are. Maybe it's just finding your way back to Him. Or maybe it's seeking Him out for the first time. Choose to be joyful every day.

Are you still wondering if God really exists? All I can do is show you from my perspective; my love of flowers and the camera. Recently, I started using a new camera and to my sheer delight, it has super macro. I have taken so many flower photos in super macro. Watch out, I am just getting started!

The great design of each of these uniquely designed flowers by the greatest designer of all time, God.

The Lord woke me up at 2:24am on the morning of July 15, 2013 to put these thoughts to paper. I did not decide what to tell you by myself. He put these words here for you to read and the photos for you to see. I am just the tool He used to touch you. To make you stop and really think about how you are doing in your life. Are you really handling things OK? Or, do you need to seek some heavenly help from our Almighty God?

It doesn't matter what church you attend to seek Him. You will know when you are at the right one for you. We each seek Him at different times in our lives and for different reasons. Are you on the right path?

My only hope for you, is that you find answers for yourself, your family, friends, and others in your community as well as those around the world in… Flowers of Hope.

Be blessed… you can be.

Paula Ann Smith

Printed in the United States
By Bookmasters